P9-CEC-194

The Understanding Your Grief
Journal

Also by Alan Wolfelt

Understanding Your Grief:
Ten Essential Touchstones for Finding Hope
and Healing Your Heart

Healing the Bereaved Child:
Grief Gardening, Growth Through Grief
and Other Touchstones for Caregivers

Healing Your Grieving Heart:
100 Practical Ideas

Healing A Friend's Grieving Heart:
100 Practical Ideas for Helping
Someone You Love Through Loss

Healing a Parent's Grieving Heart:
100 Practical Ideas After Your Child Dies

The Journey Through Grief:
Reflections On Healing

The Healing Your Grieving Heart Journal for Teens

Companion
P R E S S

Companion Press is dedicated to the education and support of both the
bereaved and bereavement caregivers. We believe that those who companion
the bereaved by walking with them as they journey in grief have a wondrous
opportunity: to help others embrace and grow through grief—and to lead fuller,
more deeply-lived lives themselves because of this important ministry.

For a complete catalog and ordering information, write or call:

Companion Press
The Center for Loss and Life Transition
3735 Broken Bow Road
Fort Collins, CO 80526
(970) 226-6050
www.centerforloss.com

The Understanding Your Grief
Journal

Exploring the Ten Essential Touchstones

A companion workbook to the book *Understanding Your Grief*

Alan D. Wolfelt, Ph.D.

Companion
PRESS

Fort Collins, Colorado
An imprint of the Center for Loss and Life Transition

© 2004 by Alan D. Wolfelt, Ph.D.

All rights reserved. No part of this publication may be reproduced,
stored in a retrieval system, or transmitted in any form or by
any means, electronic, mechanical, photocopying, recording or
otherwise, without the prior permission of the publisher.
Companion Press is an imprint of the Center for Loss and Life
Transition, 3735 Broken Bow Road, Fort Collins, Colorado 80526.

Printed in the United States of America

17 16 15 14   12 11 10

ISBN: 978-1-879651-39-5

Contents

Introduction

"Writing is the most profound way of codifying your thoughts, the best way of learning from yourself who you are and what you believe."

Warren Bennis

I have written this journal as a companion to my book *Understanding Your Grief: Ten Essential Touchstones for Finding Hope and Healing Your Heart*. My hope is that this guided journal can be a "safe place" for you to explore your experience with the ten essential touchstones.

As you tell your story, your words will guide you on your unique journey through the wilderness of your grief. Your words will also give testimony to the love you will always have for the person who has died. You can use the journal not only to understand your grief, but to remember, celebrate, and commemorate the life of the person to whom you dedicate this journal.

The Value of Journaling

Journaling has proven to be an excellent way for many people to do the work of mourning. Journaling is private and independent, yet it's still expressing your grief outside of yourself. I've been a grief counselor for a long time now (over 20 years!), and I've found that while it may not be for everyone, the process of putting the written word on paper is profoundly helpful to many grieving people in the following ways:

Journaling…

• honors the person who died.
• clarifies what you're thinking and feeling.
• creates a safe place of solace, a place where you can fully express
   yourself no matter what you are experiencing.
• allows you to tap into the touchstones of the companion book.
• helps soften the intensity of your thoughts and feelings and helps you
   better understand both your grief and your mourning.

- clears out your naturally overwhelmed mind and full heart.
- examines the pain you are experiencing and transforms it into something survivable.
- creates an opportunity to acknowledge the balance in your life between the sad and the happy.
- strengthens your awareness of how your grief journey changes over time.
- maps out your transformation as you journey through grief.

As one author observed, "When you write, you lay out a line of words. The line of words is a miner's pick, a woodcarver's gouge, a surgeon's probe. You wield it, and it digs a path you follow." To this I would add that a grief journal can provide a lifeline when you are in the midst of the wilderness. As you learn, remember, and discover new things, you can and will reach the end of your journey through grief.

Journaling Suggestions

First, please remember that there is no "correct" or "right" way to use this journal. You will not be graded on how quickly you complete the pages that follow. Actually, I would suggest that you take your time. If you are using this resource as part of a support group experience, your leaders will probably "dose" the completing of this journal over weeks or months.

If you are reading *Understanding Your Grief* and completing this journal on your own, I suggest you find a trusted person who can be available to you if and when you want to talk out any thoughts and feelings the journal brings up for you. When I say a trusted person, I mean someone who accepts you where you are right now in your grief journey. This person shouldn't judge you or think it's his or her job to "get you over" your grief quickly. Remember—there are no rewards for speed!

You will notice that in addition to the guided journal sections, in which you are asked to answer specific questions about your unique grief journey, there are a number of "Free Write" pages. These are places for you to freely write about whatever is on your heart as you are completing the journal. At the end of the journal, you will also find a section entitled "Continuing Your Journey." This is a place to write down your ongoing thoughts and feelings about the death in the years to come.

Setting
Pick a safe place to write in your journal. Naturally, journaling is usually easier to do in a quiet place that is free from interruptions and distractions.

Honesty
In an effort to open yourself to your grief and mourning, you must be honest with yourself. You must think your true thoughts and write them out, feel your true feelings and express them.

Privacy
This is your journal and yours alone. Remember—you don't have to share your journal or show it to anyone you don't want to. If you are participating in a support group, you may be invited to share some of what you write in your journal. Yet, keep in mind that sharing should always be optional, not mandatory.

Be Gentle with Yourself

Some people shy away from writing in a journal because they don't think they are good writers. It doesn't matter if you're a "good writer" or not, at least in the English teacher sense of that term. The point isn't to test your vocabulary or your punctuation or even your creative writing skills, but to explore what is on your mind and in your heart. Don't criticize what you find comes to paper. Ignore your penmanship and don't worry about grammar or spelling. This journal is for you. Journaling is a breathing space on paper. Breathe deep and go forth!

Godspeed to You

A journal is a confessor. It simply listens as you write. Believe in your ability to set your intention to heal by using the journal as one instrument in your healing. Good luck and Godspeed.

Sincerely,

Alan D. Wolfelt

Dedication

I dedicate this journal in memory of

_____
(name of the person who died)

Your name _____

*Your relationship to the person who died*_____

_____

Place a photograph below of your special person who has died:

This photo is special to me because…

_____
_____
_____
_____
_____

Getting Started
An Invitation to Open Your Heart

"Surrounded by my memories, I took my pen and began to write."
Kuki Gullman

This guided journal is a safe place for you to express your many thoughts, feelings, and memories. The purpose of this kind of guided journal is, in part, to help you learn to understand your grief and become friends with it. This resource is intended to help you open your heart and explore how someone's death has changed your life. My hope is that this journal will help you in your healing and honor your relationship with someone who has been a special part of your life here on planet Earth.

Before you begin your journey into this journal experience, please take a few minutes to reflect on where you see yourself right now at this moment in time…

Touchstone One

Open to the Presence of Your Loss

In this chapter in the companion text…

We discussed the necessity of opening to the presence of your loss. To heal in grief, you must honor—not avoid—the pain. One way to embrace the pain while at the same time maintaining hope for the future is by setting your intention to heal. Even as you embrace your pain and set your intention to heal, remember that healing in grief does not happen quickly or efficiently. Also remember that the common perception of "doing well" in grief is erroneous. To "do well" with your grief, you must not be strong and silent, but rather mourn openly and honestly.

As you were reading *Understanding Your Grief*, you discovered that honoring your grief means, in part, "remembering the value of, cherishing, and holding dear."

Describe any ways in which you have honored your grief. If you feel you have not been honoring your grief, write about ways you could begin to do so.

The pain of your grief will keep trying to get your attention until you have the courage to gently, and in small doses, embrace it. How is the pain of your grief trying to get your attention?

_____

_____

_____

_____

_____

_____

_____

_____

_____

_____

_____

_____

_____

_____

When you set your intention to heal, you make a true commitment to positively influence the course of your journey. You choose between being what I would call a "passive witness" to your grief or an "active participant" in your grief.

Describe below your understanding of the difference between being a "passive witness" to your grief or an "active participant" in your grief:

_____

_____

_____

_____

_____

_____

_____

_____

_____

Setting Your Intention to Heal

Setting Your Intention to Heal (cont.)

You learned that when you set your intention to heal, you make a true commitment to positively influence the course of your journey. Use the space below to explore your intention or intentions to heal in grief.

_____

_____

_____

_____

_____

_____

_____

_____

_____

_____

_____

_____

_____

_____

_____

_____

_____

_____

_____

_____

_____

_____

_____

_____

_____

_____

_____

_____

_____

_____

"I can continue to love while I continue to mourn." Do you agree with this statement? Why or why not?

_____

_____

_____

_____

_____

_____

_____

_____

_____

_____

_____

Making Grief Your Friend

Reconciling your grief does not happen quickly or efficiently. How do you feel about your capacity to go slow and be patient with yourself in your journey through grief?

_____

_____

_____

_____

_____

_____

_____

_____

_____

_____

_____

_____

_____

No Reward for Speed

"Doing Well" With Your Grief

Sometimes people who are openly mourning feel ashamed of their thoughts, feelings, and behaviors. Do you feel any sense of shame or embarrassment about how your grief feels or how you are mourning? If so, write about it below.

_____

_____

_____

_____

_____

_____

_____

_____

_____

_____

_____

_____

Grief Is Not A Disease

While grief is a powerful experience, so, too, is your ability to help in your own healing. Write about any steps you've taken (even baby steps!) to help yourself begin to heal.

_____

_____

_____

_____

_____

_____

_____

_____

_____

_____

_____

_____

_____

_____

Free Write

_____
_____
_____
_____
_____
_____
_____
_____
_____
_____
_____
_____
_____
_____
_____
_____
_____
_____
_____
_____
_____
_____
_____
_____
_____
_____
_____
_____
_____

Touchstone Two
Dispel the Misconceptions About Grief

In this chapter in the companion text…

We discovered that many of the perceptions we may have had—and society often teaches us—about grief and mourning aren't true at all. For example, grief does NOT progress in predictable, orderly stages. And tears aren't a sign of weakness; actually, they're a form of mourning and they are natural and necessary. Many misconceptions color our expectations about grief. The trick is to sort out the fact from the fiction and grieve and mourn in healthy, authentic ways.

Misconception 1: Grief and mourning are the same thing.

Did you used to think that grief and mourning were the same thing? If so, how has this misconception affected you?

_____

_____

_____

_____

_____

_____

_____

_____

_____

_____

_____

_____

_____

_____

_____

_____

_____

_____

_____

_____

_____

_____

_____

_____

_____

_____

_____

_____

_____

_____

_____

_____

_____

_____

_____

Now that we've explored the difference between grief and mourning, how will you mourn this death—that is, openly and honestly express your grief outside of yourself?

_____

_____

_____

_____

_____

_____

_____

_____

_____

_____

Do you see yourself having difficulty with expressing your grief outside of yourself (mourning) in any ways? If so, what ways?

_____

_____

_____

_____

_____

_____

_____

_____

_____

_____

_____

_____

_____

_____

Have you heard about the "stages of grief"? If so, what is or was your feeling about this popular grief model?

Misconception 2: Grief and mourning progress in predictable, orderly stages.

_____

_____

_____

_____

_____

_____

_____

_____

_____

_____

_____

_____

_____

_____

_____

_____

_____

_____

_____

_____

_____

_____

_____

_____

_____

_____

_____

_____

_____

_____

_____

_____

Now that you've learned that "stages" in grief aren't orderly and predictable, how do you believe you will move forward in your own unique journey through grief?

_____

_____

_____

_____

_____

_____

_____

_____

_____

_____

_____

Grief is often a one step forward, two steps back process. How could you help yourself during those inevitable times when you think you're moving backwards instead of forward?

_____

_____

_____

_____

_____

_____

_____

_____

_____

_____

_____

_____

_____

Have you felt pressured to "overcome" your grief instead of experiencing it? If so, how and why have you been pressured?

_____

_____

_____

_____

_____

_____

_____

_____

_____

_____

_____

_____

What does it mean to you to move toward your pain?

_____

_____

_____

_____

_____

_____

_____

_____

_____

_____

_____

_____

_____

_____

Misconception 3: You should move away from grief, not toward it.

How could you respond to friends, family, coworkers, etc. who encourage you (either outright or implicitly) to move away from your grief?

_____

_____

_____

_____

_____

_____

_____

_____

_____

_____

Have you cried since the death? If so, in what circumstances and how often? If not, why not?

_____

_____

_____

_____

_____

_____

_____

_____

_____

_____

_____

_____

_____

Misconception 3 (cont.)

Misconception 4: Tears of grief are only a sign of weakness.

Misconception 4 (cont.)

Do others around you make you feel a sense of shame or weakness about crying? If so, who and why?

_____
_____
_____
_____
_____
_____
_____
_____
_____
_____
_____
_____
_____
_____
_____
_____
_____

Do you yourself feel a sense of shame or weakness about crying? If so, what can you do to help yourself understand that tears are a normal, even necessary, form of mourning?

_____
_____
_____
_____
_____
_____
_____
_____
_____
_____
_____
_____

Are you a person of faith? Do you believe in God or a power greater than yourself? Whether your answer is yes or no, write about your personal beliefs.

_____

_____

_____

_____

_____

_____

_____

_____

_____

_____

_____

_____

_____

_____

_____

_____

_____

_____

_____

_____

_____

_____

_____

_____

_____

_____

Misconception 5: Being "upset" and openly mourning means you are being "weak" in your faith.

Misconception 5 (cont.)

Do you think you are being weak in your faith if you are struggling with this death? Or has anyone else made you feel this way? Write about your understanding of the relationship between healthy mourning and having faith.

_____

_____

_____

_____

_____

_____

_____

_____

_____

_____

_____

_____

_____

_____

_____

_____

_____

_____

_____

_____

_____

_____

_____

_____

_____

_____

_____

_____

_____

_____

Since the death, you may have realized that there are many things you have lost besides the company of the person who died. List the secondary losses you are experiencing as a result of the death.

_____   _____   _____

_____   _____   _____

_____   _____   _____

_____   _____   _____

_____   _____   _____

_____   _____   _____

_____   _____   _____

From the above list, choose one or two of your most hurtful or significant secondary losses and write about them here.

_____

_____

_____

_____

_____

_____

_____

_____

_____

_____

_____

_____

_____

_____

_____

_____

Misconception 6: When someone you love dies, you only grieve and mourn for the physical loss of the person.

27

Since the death, have you encountered a holiday, anniversary date, or birthday that was connected to the person who died? Describe what you did on this day and how you felt.

Misconception 7: You should try not to think about the person who died on holidays, anniversaries, and birthdays.

On this day, did you try to avoid thinking about the person who died or did you try to honor your grief and the memory of the person who died? Write about your choice and how it turned out for you.

_____

_____

_____

_____

_____

_____

_____

_____

_____

_____

Misconception 7 (cont.)

What is the next upcoming holiday, anniversary, or birthday connected to the person who died? How could you commemorate the life of the person who died on this day?

_____

_____

_____

_____

_____

_____

_____

_____

_____

_____

_____

_____

_____

_____

Are you hoping to "get over" your grief? If so, why? If not, why not?

Misconception 8: After someone you love dies, the goal should be to "get over" your grief as soon as possible.

_____

_____

_____

_____

_____

_____

_____

_____

_____

_____

_____

_____

_____

_____

_____

_____

_____

_____

_____

_____

_____

_____

_____

_____

_____

_____

_____

_____

_____

_____

_____

Has anyone else told you or made you feel that you need to "get over" your grief ? If so, who and in what circumstances? How did this make you feel?

_____

_____

_____

_____

_____

_____

_____

_____

_____

_____

_____

How do you feel about the reality that you do not get over your grief but rather learn to reconcile yourself to it?

_____

_____

_____

_____

_____

_____

_____

_____

_____

_____

_____

_____

Are you normally an independent person who does everything for him/herself or are you an interdependent person who relies on others for help with some things? Explain.

_____

_____

_____

_____

_____

_____

_____

_____

_____

_____

In order to heal, you will need to reach out to others to help you with your grief. Do you believe this to be true? Why or why not?

_____

_____

_____

_____

_____

_____

_____

_____

_____

List at least three people who would be naturally good companions for you on your journey through the wilderness of your grief.

_____

_____

_____

Misconception 9: Nobody can help you with your grief.

This misconception is a close cousin to Misconception 8, which says that your goal should be to "get over" your grief as soon as possible. Grief doesn't end, but it does erupt less frequently. Have you had any recent "eruptions" you could write about?

_____
_____
_____
_____
_____
_____
_____
_____

Do you have any "grief role models" in your life—people who mourned openly and honestly after a death and went on to reconcile their grief and continue to live a life of meaning and joy? If so, who? How does this person (or these people) continue to acknowledge and honor his or her grief in the years and decades after the death?

_____
_____
_____
_____
_____
_____
_____
_____
_____
_____
_____
_____

Misconception 10: When grief and mourning are finally reconciled, they never come up again.

Use the space below to write out any additional misconceptions you have experienced or observed and the ways in which they have thus far influenced your grief journey.

Free Write

Touchstone Three

Embrace the Uniqueness of Your Grief

In this chapter in the companion text…

We developed an understanding that each person's grief is unique and that grief and mourning can never be strictly compared. We also explored all the many reasons that your grief is *your* grief—why it is unique to you and unlike anyone else's.

Why #1: Your relationship with the person who died

If someone asked you to describe your relationship with the person who died, what would immediately come to your head and your heart?

_____

_____

_____

_____

_____

_____

_____

_____

_____

_____

_____

_____

_____

_____

_____

_____

How attached were you to this person?

_____

_____

_____

_____

_____

_____

_____

_____

_____

Describe how you acted and felt in one another's company.

_____

_____

_____

_____

_____

_____

_____

_____

_____

_____

_____

_____

Can you remember a time when you felt very close to this person?
Please describe it here.

_____

_____

_____

_____

_____

_____

_____

_____

_____

_____

_____

_____

_____

_____

_____

Why #1 (cont.)

Were there times when it was difficult to get along with this person? If so, give some examples of those times. If not, write about why you think you got along so well.

_____

_____

_____

_____

_____

_____

_____

_____

_____

_____

_____

_____

_____

_____

What did the person who died look like?
Approximate height_____ Approximate weight_____
Hair color_____ Eye color_____

Other distinguishing characteristics:

_____

_____

_____

_____

_____

_____

_____

_____

_____

_____

Write about two special memories you will always have of your
relationship with the person who died.

_____

_____

_____

_____

_____

_____

_____

_____

_____

_____

_____

_____

_____

_____

_____

_____

_____

_____

_____

_____

_____

_____

_____

_____

_____

_____

_____

_____

_____

Why #1 (cont.)

Why #2: The circumstances of the death

Describe the circumstances of the death.

_____

_____

_____

_____

_____

_____

_____

_____

_____

_____

How did you learn about the death?

_____

_____

_____

_____

_____

_____

_____

Was the death something you expected to happen or was it sudden and unexpected? How does the answer to this question affect your grief?

_____

_____

_____

_____

_____

_____

_____

_____

How old was the person who died? _____
Is the person's age affecting your grief? If so, how?

_____

_____

_____

_____

_____

_____

What questions, if any, do you still have about how or why the person died?

_____

_____

_____

_____

_____

Is there someone you could talk to who could help work these questions out?

_____

_____

What other thoughts and feelings come to mind when you think about how this person died?

_____

_____

_____

_____

_____

_____

_____

_____

_____

_____

Why #2 (cont.)

Why #3: The ritual or funeral experience

Did you plan and/or attend a funeral for the person who died? If so, describe what this experience was like for you.

_____

_____

_____

_____

_____

_____

_____

_____

_____

_____

_____

_____

_____

_____

_____

_____

_____

_____

_____

_____

_____

_____

_____

_____

_____

_____

_____

If you were not able to be a part of the funeral, how do you feel about that?

_____

_____

_____

_____

_____

_____

_____

_____

_____

Do you think it would be helpful for you to create an additional ritual to help you and others heal? What ideas do you have for creating a ceremony?

_____

_____

_____

_____

_____

_____

_____

_____

_____

In what ways can you continue to use ceremony to remember other special times, such as the birthday of the person who died or the anniversary of the death?

_____

_____

_____

_____

_____

Why #4: The people in your life

Do you have people in your life (friends and family) whom you can turn to for help and support? Who? List them.

_____

_____

_____

_____

_____

What qualities do these people have that make them able to "walk with" you in your grief?

_____

_____

_____

_____

_____

_____

Are there people in your life you could turn to for support but for some reason you don't feel you can? If so, who and why?

_____

_____

_____

_____

_____

_____

Are you willing to accept support from friends and family? If not, why not?

_____

_____

_____

_____

_____

_____

Sometimes well-meaning friends and family will hurt you unknowingly with their words. They may tell you:

- "I know how you feel." (They don't.)
- "Get on with your life." (You're not ready to.)
- "Keep your chin up." (You have every right to be sad.)
- "Time heals all wounds." (Time helps, but it alone doesn't heal.)
- "He/she wouldn't want you to be sad." (Maybe not, but he/she would also understand why you are!)

Have you had anyone say things like this to you? If so, write out an example and describe how it made you feel.

_____

_____

_____

_____

_____

_____

_____

What are some things that people have said or done that have been helpful to you?

_____

_____

_____

_____

_____

Do you have friends at work, at your place of worship, and/or at an organization you are a part of who are supportive of your grief? Who are these people and how can you continue to reach out to them?

_____

_____

_____

_____

_____

Why #4 (cont.)

Why #4 (cont.)

Are you attending a support group as you work through this journal and companion text? If so, can you describe how this group experience is going for you so far?

_____

_____

_____

_____

_____

_____

_____

_____

_____

_____

_____

_____

_____

Are you seeing a counselor who is helping you work through this journal and companion text? If so, what has the counseling experience been like for you so far?

_____

_____

_____

_____

_____

_____

_____

_____

_____

_____

_____

_____

What are some adjectives you would use to describe yourself?

_____   _____

_____   _____

_____   _____

_____   _____

How do you think your unique personality is influencing your grief and mourning?

_____

_____

_____

_____

_____

_____

_____

_____

_____

_____

_____

_____

_____

_____

How have you responded to other life losses or crises in your life?

_____

_____

_____

_____

_____

_____

_____

_____

Why #5: Your unique personality

Why #5 (cont.)

Are you responding in a similar way now, or does this loss feel different? Explain.

_____

_____

_____

_____

Do you think your personality has changed as a result of this death? If so, how? If not, why not?

_____

_____

_____

_____

_____

_____

_____

How is your self-esteem right now?

_____

_____

_____

_____

_____

_____

_____

Do you think this death has impacted how you feel about yourself? If so, how?

_____

_____

_____

_____

_____

_____

Check off the following personality traits that seem to describe the person who died.

___ accepting	___ active	___ adventuresome
___ aggressive	___ annoying	___ anxious
___ argumentative	___ artistic	___ big-hearted
___ calm	___ caring	___ charming
___ clever	___ cold	___ compassionate
___ competitive	___ conceited	___ confident
___ controlling	___ cooperative	___ courageous
___ creative	___ critical	___ demanding
___ dependable	___ detached	___ direct
___ dramatic	___ dynamic	___ emotional
___ energetic	___ enthusiastic	___ fair
___ forgetful	___ friendly	___ funny
___ good-natured	___ graceful	___ honest
___ hyperactive	___ imaginative	___ independent
___ inflexible	___ influential	___ insecure
___ interesting	___ inventive	___ irritable
___ jealous	___ logical	___ loud
___ moody	___ nervous	___ nurturing
___ opinionated	___ outgoing	___ overprotective
___ overwhelming	___ perfectionistic	___ persuasive
___ playful	___ protective	___ punctual
___ quick to anger	___ rebellious	___ resourceful
___ rude	___ romantic	___ scatterbrained
___ self-centered	___ sensitive	___ shy
___ sincere	___ smart	___ spiritual
___ spontaneous	___ stubborn	___ temperamental
___ tireless	___ troubled	___ trustworthy
___ two-faced	___ warm	___ wise
___ witty	___ wonderful	___ worried

Why #6 (cont.) Now, in your own words, describe the personality of the person who died.

_____
_____
_____
_____
_____
_____
_____
_____
_____
_____
_____
_____
_____
_____
_____
_____
_____
_____
_____
_____
_____
_____
_____
_____
_____
_____
_____
_____
_____
_____

Place a photo of the person who died here, one that you think expresses his or her unique personality.

Why #6 (cont.)

What roles did this person play in your life? (For example, husband, best friend, advisor, lover, anchor, etc.)

_____

_____

_____

_____

How did this person's unique personality affect the roles he or she played in your life?

_____

_____

_____

_____

_____

_____

_____

_____

_____

_____

_____

_____

_____

What personality traits of this person did you enjoy the most?

_____

_____

_____

_____

_____

_____

_____

_____

Give an example of a time when these personality traits really shone through in this person.

_____

_____

_____

_____

_____

_____

_____

What personality traits of this person's did you least enjoy?

_____

_____

_____

_____

Give an example of a time when these negative traits were apparent to you.

_____

_____

_____

_____

_____

_____

_____

If you were asked to list the three personality traits you admired the most in this person, what would those be? (You might want to review the checklist on p. 51.)

_____

_____

_____

Why #7: Your gender

Do you think that being a man or a woman affects your grief? If so, how? If not, why not?

_____

_____

_____

_____

_____

_____

_____

_____

Has your gender influenced how people support you in your grief? If so, how?

_____

_____

_____

_____

_____

_____

_____

_____

_____

In grief, do you see any advantages or disadvantages to being the gender you are?

_____

_____

_____

_____

_____

_____

_____

_____

_____

What is your cultural background?

_____

_____

_____

_____

_____

How does this background influence your grief and mourning?

_____

_____

_____

_____

If you were asked to articulate them, what would you say some of your family's "rules" were about coping with loss and grief? In what ways did you see these rules carried out?

_____

_____

_____

_____

_____

_____

_____

_____

How do you feel about these rules and their helpfulness to you (or unhelpfulness to you) in grief?

_____

_____

_____

_____

Why #8: Your cultural background

Why #9: Your religious or spiritual background

Did you grow up with certain religious or spiritual teachings? Please describe them.

_____

_____

_____

_____

_____

_____

_____

_____

_____

_____

_____

_____

Have your religious or spiritual beliefs changed over time? If so, describe how they have changed.

_____

_____

_____

_____

_____

_____

_____

_____

_____

_____

_____

_____

_____

_____

_____

How has this death affected your belief system? Be specific.

_____

_____

_____

_____

_____

_____

_____

_____

_____

_____

_____

_____

_____

_____

_____

_____

_____

_____

_____

_____

_____

_____

_____

_____

_____

_____

_____

_____

_____

Why #9 (cont.)

Do you have people around you who understand and support you in your belief system? If so, who are these people and how can they help you now?

_____

_____

_____

_____

Do you think that your faith, religion or spiritual background is playing a part in your healing process? Please explain.

_____

_____

_____

_____

_____

_____

_____

_____

_____

_____

_____

Why #10: Other crises or stresses in your life right now

What other losses have come about in your life either as a result of the death or coincidentally during the same time frame?

_____

_____

_____

_____

_____

_____

_____

_____

_____

How do you see these other losses influencing your grief?

_____

_____

_____

_____

_____

_____

_____

What other stresses or crises are a part of your life right now?

_____

_____

_____

_____

_____

_____

_____

How are they affecting your grief?

_____

_____

_____

_____

_____

Whom can you turn to right now to help you cope with these secondary losses or stresses?

_____

_____

_____

_____

Why #11: Your experience with loss and death in the past

Have you had other significant death losses in your life? If so, please describe them.

_____

_____

_____

_____

_____

_____

_____

_____

Compared to these previous grief journeys, how does this grief journey feel for you and why?

_____

_____

_____

_____

_____

_____

_____

_____

Have you experienced any significant non-death losses in your life, such as divorce, job loss, etc? If so, write them down and consider how they might now be affecting your grief.

_____

_____

_____

_____

_____

_____

_____

You'll be writing more about this on p. 110 of this journal. For now, take a moment to write about how you are feeling physically right now.

Why #12: Your physical health

_____

_____

_____

_____

_____

_____

_____

_____

_____

_____

_____

_____

Are there other factors, large or small, that are influencing your grief right now? If so, write about them here.

Other Whys

_____

_____

_____

_____

_____

_____

_____

_____

_____

_____

_____

_____

_____

_____

_____

_____

_____

Free Write

_____
_____
_____
_____
_____
_____
_____
_____
_____
_____
_____
_____
_____
_____
_____
_____
_____
_____
_____
_____
_____
_____
_____
_____
_____
_____
_____
_____
_____

Touchstone Four

Explore Your Feelings of Loss

In this chapter in the companion text…

We agreed that as strange as your emotions may seem, they are a true
expression of where you are right now in your journey through grief.
We emphasized that whatever your grief thoughts and feelings are, they
are normal and necessary. Feelings aren't right or wrong, they just are.
Naming the feelings and acknowledging them are the first steps to
dealing with them. It's actually the process of becoming friendly with
your feelings that will help you heal.

Before exploring some of your possible responses to the death of your special person, please take a moment to write out a few words that describe how you are feeling right now. In the space below, complete the following statement:

Right now, I'm feeling...

_____

_____

_____

_____

_____

_____

_____

_____

_____

_____

_____

Shock, Numbness, Denial, and Disbelief

Have you felt "in shock" or "numb" since the death? What was this like for you?

_____

_____

_____

_____

_____

_____

_____

_____

_____

_____

_____

_____

_____

Do you feel like your shock and numbness helped you through the early days after the death? If yes, how? If no, why not?

_____

_____

_____

_____

_____

_____

_____

_____

_____

_____

_____

_____

Do you feel that you are or have been in denial about the death? Please explain.

_____

_____

_____

_____

_____

_____

_____

_____

_____

_____

_____

_____

_____

_____

_____

_____

Shock, Numbness, Denial, and Disbelief (cont.)

Are you learning to allow yourself to acknowledge the death in small doses in between your periods of denial? In the companion book, I called this EVADE ◄─► ENCOUNTER. If you are stuck on EVADE, how can you help yourself ENCOUNTER the reality of the death?

_____

_____

_____

_____

_____

_____

_____

How have your feelings of shock, numbness, denial, and disbelief changed or softened since the death?

_____

_____

_____

_____

_____

_____

_____

What are you doing to express your feelings of shock, numbness, denial, and disbelief?

_____

_____

_____

_____

_____

_____

_____

In the companion book, I explained that you may feel a sense of rest-lessness, agitation, impatience, and ongoing confusion. Have you felt these feelings and if so, what have they been like for you?

_____

_____

_____

_____

_____

_____

_____

_____

Disorganization, Confusion, Searching, Yearning

Do you keep starting tasks but never finishing them? Do you forget what you are saying mid-sentence? Are you having trouble getting through your day-to-day commitments? Name some ways in which your grief feelings of disorganization and confusion are affecting your life.

_____

_____

_____

_____

_____

_____

_____

Have you experienced a yearning or searching for the person who died? Please explain.

_____

_____

_____

_____

_____

Do you think you've "seen" or "heard" the person who has died? If so, write about this experience.

_____

_____

_____

_____

_____

_____

_____

_____

_____

Do you dream about the person who died? Describe your dreams.

_____

_____

_____

_____

_____

_____

_____

_____

What are you doing to express your feelings of disorganization, confusion, searching, and yearning?

_____

_____

_____

_____

_____

_____

_____

_____

_____

Have you felt anxious, panicked, or fearful since the death? If so, please explain.

_____

_____

_____

_____

_____

_____

_____

_____

Anxiety, Panic, Fear

What are you most afraid of since the death?

_____

_____

_____

_____

_____

_____

_____

_____

What are you doing to express your feelings of anxiety, panic, and fear?

_____

_____

_____

_____

_____

_____

_____

_____

Explosive Emotions

Have you felt anger, hate, blame, terror, resentment, rage, and/or jealousy about the death? If not, write about why you think these feelings haven't been a part of your grief journey so far. If so, which of these feelings have you experienced? List them in the left column then write more about them in the right column.

_____   _____
                                   _____
                                   _____
                                   _____
                                   _____
                                   _____
                                   _____
                                   _____
                                   _____
_____   _____
                                   _____
                                   _____
                                   _____
                                   _____
                                   _____
                                   _____
                                   _____
                                   _____
_____   _____
                                   _____
                                   _____
                                   _____
                                   _____
                                   _____
                                   _____
                                   _____

Have others around you been upset by your expression of these feelings? Explain.

_____

_____

_____

_____

_____

_____

_____

_____

_____

_____

_____

Explosive Emotions (cont.)

What are you doing to express your explosive emotions in healthy ways?

_____

_____

_____

_____

_____

_____

_____

_____

_____

_____

_____

_____

_____

_____

Guilt and Regret

Have you had a case of the "if-onlys" since the death? If so, write about your if-onlys and how they make you feel.

_____

_____

_____

_____

_____

_____

_____

_____

_____

_____

_____

_____

_____

Do you think you have any of the following specific subtypes of guilt?

Survivor guilt   Relief-guilt   Joy-guilt

Magical thinking and guilt   Longstanding guilt

I invite you to circle the kinds of guilt that apply to you, if any, and write about them below.

_____

_____

_____

_____

_____

_____

_____

_____

_____

_____

_____

_____

_____

_____

_____

How do other people make you feel about your feelings of guilt and regret?

_____

_____

_____

_____

_____

_____

_____

_____

_____

_____

_____

_____

_____

What are you doing to express your guilt and regret?

_____

_____

_____

_____

_____

_____

_____

_____

_____

_____

_____

_____

_____

Guilt and Regret (cont.)

Sadness and Depression

How sad are you feeling about the death right now? How does this compare to the sadness you may have felt earlier in your grief journey?

_____

_____

_____

_____

_____

_____

_____

_____

_____

_____

_____

_____

Are there certain days or times of day that are saddest for you now? Explain.

_____

_____

_____

_____

_____

_____

_____

When you start feeling sad, what can you do to help yourself embrace your sadness instead of moving away from it?

_____

_____

_____

_____

_____

_____

Have you had any thoughts of suicide since the death? If so, please explain.

_____

_____

_____

_____

_____

_____

_____

_____

Keep in mind that transient, passive thoughts of suicide in grief are normal but that persistent, active thoughts of suicide are not. If you are actively considering or making plans to take your own life, put down this journal this very moment and call someone who will help you get help. If this is an emergency, call 911 immediately.

What are you doing to express your sadness and depression?

_____

_____

_____

_____

_____

_____

_____

Do you think you might be clinically depressed instead of just grieving? If yes, review the chart on page 65 in the companion book and determine if you meet any of the criteria for clinical depression. Do you exhibit any of the listed characteristics of clinical depression? If yes, write down your physician's name and phone number in the space below then put down this journal, go to the phone, and make an appointment to see him or her as soon as possible. Remember that getting help for your depression does not mean you are weak, it means you are strong.

_____

Sadness and Depression (cont.)

Clinical Depression

Relief and Release

Did you feel a sense of relief after the death? If yes, why?

_____

_____

_____

_____

_____

_____

_____

_____

_____

_____

_____

_____

_____

How do you feel about feeling relieved? Do you think it's OK or not OK?

_____

_____

_____

_____

_____

_____

_____

_____

_____

_____

_____

_____

_____

_____

What are you doing to express your feelings of relief and release?

_____

_____

_____

_____

_____

_____

_____

_____

_____

_____

Are you having other feelings that haven't been covered in this discussion? Please take a few minutes to explain them here.

_____

_____

_____

_____

_____

_____

_____

_____

_____

_____

_____

_____

_____

Free Write

Touchstone Five
Recognize You Are Not Crazy

In this chapter in the companion text…

We discussed the common feeling people in grief have that they are going crazy. Many of the thoughts and feelings you will experience in your journey through grief are so different from your everyday reality that you may feel you're going crazy. You're not. You're just grieving. The two can feel remarkably similar sometimes. This chapter also explores a number of typical thoughts and feelings that contribute to the feeling of going crazy in grief.

Time Distortion

Has time seemed distorted to you since the death? Explain.

_____
_____
_____
_____
_____
_____
_____
_____
_____
_____
_____
_____
_____

Self-Focus

Have you felt the need to focus on yourself and pay less attention to others in your journey through grief? Explain.

_____
_____
_____
_____
_____
_____
_____
_____
_____
_____
_____
_____
_____

Are you re-thinking and/or re-telling the story of the death over and over again? If so, what is it exactly that you are feeling the need to think about and/or talk about? Describe it here.

_____

_____

_____

_____

_____

_____

_____

_____

_____

_____

_____

_____

_____

_____

_____

_____

_____

_____

_____

_____

_____

_____

_____

_____

_____

_____

Re-thinking and Re-telling the Story

Sudden Changes In Mood

Have you been moody since the death? Please explain.

_____

_____

_____

_____

_____

_____

_____

_____

_____

_____

_____

_____

_____

Powerlessness and Helplessness

Has this death made you feel powerless or helpless? In what ways?

_____

_____

_____

_____

_____

_____

_____

_____

_____

_____

_____

_____

_____

_____

_____

Have you had any griefbursts since the death? If yes, describe where you were and what happened.

_____

_____

_____

_____

_____

_____

_____

_____

_____

_____

_____

_____

Grief Attacks or Griefbursts

Do you find yourself expressing your grief by crying a lot? If so, how do you feel each time after you're done crying? If not, why do you think you're not crying?

_____

_____

_____

_____

_____

_____

_____

_____

_____

_____

_____

Crying and Sobbing

Linking Objects

Do you have any linking objects that belonged to or remind you of the person who died? If yes, list them here and describe how they make you feel. If not, why not?

_____

_____

_____

_____

_____

_____

_____

_____

_____

_____

Identification Symptoms of Physical Illness

Have you found yourself experiencing any physical symptoms similar to those of the person who died? If yes, describe them and explain how you feel about these symptoms.

_____

_____

_____

_____

_____

_____

_____

_____

_____

Would it make you feel better to see a physician about these symptoms? If yes, call your physician for an appointment right now and note the time and date of the appointment here.

_____

_____

Have you contemplated suicide since the death? If yes, write more about your thoughts here. Also, please see page 77 of this journal for more on suicidal thoughts and determining if they are dangerous.

_____

_____

_____

_____

_____

_____

_____

_____

_____

_____

_____

_____

_____

Suicidal Thoughts

Have you been using drugs or alcohol to dull your painful feelings of grief? If yes, describe what your use habits have been.

_____

_____

_____

_____

_____

_____

_____

_____

_____

_____

_____

_____

Drugs, Alcohol, and Grief

Dreams

Have you had any pleasant dreams about the person who died? If so, describe them here.

_____

_____

_____

_____

_____

_____

_____

_____

Have you had any unpleasant dreams or nightmares about the person who died? If so, describe them here.

_____

_____

_____

_____

_____

_____

_____

Mystical Experiences

Have you had any mystical experiences that you believe are some form of communication from the person who died? If yes, write about your mystical experiences and how they made you feel in the space below.

_____

_____

_____

_____

_____

_____

_____

In general, have you had a tough time coping on anniversaries, birthdays, or holidays since the death? Write about your experience here.

Anniversary and Holiday Grief Occasions

Free Write

_____
_____
_____
_____
_____
_____
_____
_____
_____
_____
_____
_____
_____
_____
_____
_____
_____
_____
_____
_____
_____
_____
_____
_____
_____
_____
_____
_____
_____
_____
_____
_____
_____

Touchstone Six

Understand the Six Needs of Mourning

In this chapter in the companion text...

We introduced the six needs of mourning, which are the six central needs that all mourners must meet in order to heal. Remember, the six needs are not orderly or predictable. You will probably jump around in random fashion while working on them, and you will address each need only when you are ready to do so.

Mourning Need 1: Accept the reality of the death.

Where do you see yourself in accepting the reality of this death?

_____

_____

_____

_____

_____

_____

_____

_____

Do you think time is playing a part in where you are with this need? If so, how?

_____

_____

_____

_____

_____

Do you understand and allow yourself the need to at times push some of the reality away? If so, how?

_____

_____

_____

_____

_____

_____

_____

_____

What can you do to continue to work on this need?

_____

_____

_____

_____

Where do you see yourself in allowing yourself to feel the pain of the loss?

_____

_____

_____

_____

Do you think that time is playing a part in where you are with this need? If so, how?

_____

_____

_____

_____

With whom have you shared your feelings of hurt?

_____

_____

_____

Write about what sharing your feelings has been like for you.

_____

_____

_____

What can you do to continue to work on this need?

_____

_____

_____

Mourning Need 2: Let yourself feel the pain of the loss.

Mourning Need 3: Remember the person who died.

If you have another favorite picture of the person who died, place it here in your journal:

Where do you see yourself in the process of remembering the person who died?

_____

_____

_____

_____

_____

_____

_____

_____

Write out below a funny or meaningful story about the person who died.

_____

_____

_____

_____

_____

_____

_____

_____

_____

_____

_____

_____

_____

_____

_____

_____

_____

_____

Mourning Need 3 (cont.)

What do you miss the very most about the person who died?

_____

_____

_____

_____

_____

_____

What do you miss the least about the person who died?

_____

_____

_____

_____

_____

_____

What other things will you always remember about the person who died?

_____

_____

_____

_____

_____

_____

What would you want others to always remember about the person who died?

_____

_____

_____

_____

_____

_____

_____

Sayings the person who died used to say are . . .

_____

_____

_____

_____

_____

_____

_____

_____

_____

_____

The most important thing I learned from the person who died was...

_____

_____

_____

_____

_____

_____

_____

_____

_____

_____

_____

_____

_____

_____

_____

_____

_____

_____

Mourning Need 3 (cont.)

In the space below, write a letter to the person who died. Tell him or her what is in your head and on your heart.

Dear _____,

_____

_____

_____

_____

_____

_____

_____

_____

_____

_____

_____

_____

_____

_____

_____

_____

_____

_____

_____

_____

_____

_____

_____

_____

_____

_____

_____

_____

In the space below, imagine the person who died could write a letter back to you. What do you think he or she would want to say to you?

Dear _____,

_____

_____

_____

_____

_____

_____

_____

_____

_____

_____

_____

_____

_____

_____

_____

_____

_____

_____

_____

_____

_____

What can you do to continue to work on this need?

_____

_____

_____

_____

Mourning Need 4: Develop a new self-identity.

Where do you see yourself in developing a new self-identity?

_____
_____
_____
_____
_____
_____
_____
_____
_____
_____
_____

What roles did the person who died play in your life?

_____
_____
_____
_____
_____
_____
_____
_____

What identity changes have you experienced as a result of this death?

_____
_____
_____
_____
_____
_____
_____
_____

How do you see people treating you differently as a result of your changed identity?

_____

_____

_____

_____

_____

_____

_____

_____

_____

Which, if any, positive changes in your self-identity have you noticed since the death?

_____

_____

_____

_____

_____

_____

_____

_____

_____

_____

What can you do to continue to work on this need?

_____

_____

_____

_____

_____

_____

Mourning Need 5: Search for meaning.

Where do you see yourself in your search for meaning?

_____

_____

_____

_____

_____

_____

Do you have any "Why?" or "How?" questions right now? If so, what
are they?

_____

_____

_____

_____

_____

_____

_____

Are you wrestling with your faith right now? Explain.

_____

_____

_____

_____

_____

_____

_____

_____

_____

_____

_____

_____

What can you do to continue to work on this need?

_____

_____

_____

_____

Studies have shown that prayer can help people heal. If you believe in a higher power, the space below is a safe place for you to write out a prayer. You might pray about the person who died or about your questions about life and death. You might pray for help in dealing with the pain you feel. You might pray for others affected by this death. Pray for anything that is on your grieving heart.

Dear God,

_____

_____

_____

_____

_____

_____

_____

_____

_____

_____

_____

_____

_____

_____

_____

_____

_____

_____

Mourning Need 6: Let others help you—now and always.

Where do you see yourself in letting others help you—now and always?

_____
_____
_____
_____
_____
_____
_____
_____
_____
_____
_____
_____

Whom do you turn to for help?

_____
_____
_____
_____
_____

What do these people do that lets you know they are there to support you?

_____
_____
_____
_____
_____
_____
_____
_____
_____
_____

How are you doing at accepting support from people who try to give it?

_____

_____

_____

_____

_____

_____

Are you getting support from others who have experienced the death of someone loved? Please explain.

_____

_____

_____

_____

_____

_____

_____

_____

_____

_____

_____

_____

What can you do to continue to work on this need?

_____

_____

_____

_____

_____

_____

_____

Free Write

Touchstone Seven
Nurture Yourself

In this chapter in the companion text…

We reminded ourselves of the need to be self-nurturing in grief.
Remember—self-care fortifies you for your long and challenging grief
journey. In nurturing ourselves, in allowing ourselves the time and
loving attention we need to journey safely and deeply through grief, we
find meaning in our continued living. We then explored the five realms
in which it is critical to nurture ourselves: physical; emotional;
cognitive; social; and spiritual.

The Mourner's Code is a list of ten basic principles that empower you on your journey to healing. Below you are invited to write about how each principle applies to your unique grief.

1. You have the right to experience your own unique grief.

_____

_____

_____

_____

2. You have the right to talk about your grief.

_____

_____

_____

_____

3. You have the right to feel a multitude of emotions.

_____

_____

_____

_____

4. You have the right to be tolerant of your physical and emotional limits.

_____

_____

_____

_____

5. You have the right to experience "griefbursts."

_____

_____

_____

_____

The Mourner's Code

6.You have the right to make use of ritual.

_____

_____

_____

_____

7.You have the right to embrace your spirituality.

_____

_____

_____

_____

8.You have the right to search for meaning.

_____

_____

_____

_____

9.You have the right to treasure your memories.

_____

_____

_____

_____

10.You have the right to move toward your grief and heal.

_____

_____

_____

_____

The Mourner's Code (cont.)

Nurturing Yourself: The Physical Realm

Is your body letting you know that it feels distressed right now? If so, how?

_____

_____

_____

_____

_____

_____

How are you sleeping?

_____

_____

_____

_____

How are you eating?

_____

_____

_____

_____

Of the Twelve Commandments of Good Health (pp. 107-110), which do you feel you are following right now? List them here.

_____

_____

_____

_____

_____

_____

_____

_____

How do you give attention to your thoughts and feelings in grief?

_____

_____

_____

_____

_____

_____

Do you have physical contact with other human beings? If yes, describe how it makes you feel. If no, why not?

_____

_____

_____

_____

_____

_____

_____

_____

What kinds of music touch your heart and soul? List your favorite artists and types of music here. You might also mention music that was important to the person who died.

_____

_____

_____

_____

_____

_____

Nurturing Yourself: The Emotional Realm

The Emotional Realm (cont.) Draw a grief map here. Make a circle at the center of the page and label it MY GRIEF. This circle represents your thoughts and feelings since the death. Now draw lines radiating out of this circle and label each line with a thought or feeling that has contributed to your grief. If you don't have room on this page to make your grief map, get a big piece of paper and do it there. Remember—you will not be graded for your artistic abilities. Just do it!

What gives you pleasure and joy in your life? Write down 10 things.

_____

_____

_____

_____

_____

_____

_____

_____

_____

_____

The Emotional Realm (cont.)

Does your ability to think and concentrate seem to be affected by your grief? If so, how?

_____

_____

_____

_____

_____

Nurturing Yourself: The Cognitive Realm

Now that this person has died, what do you want in life? What is wanted of you? Answer these two questions in the space below.

_____

_____

_____

_____

_____

_____

_____

_____

The Cognitive Realm (cont.)

Make a list of goals for the coming year. Be reasonable and compassionate with yourself in determining these goals.

_____

_____

_____

_____

_____

_____

_____

_____

_____

_____

_____

Count your blessings. What do you still have to be thankful for in your life? Make a gratitude list here.

_____

_____

_____

_____

_____

_____

_____

_____

_____

_____

_____

_____

_____

_____

_____

_____

How are you making an effort to stay connected to other people in your life?

_____

_____

_____

_____

_____

_____

_____

Have your friendships changed since the death? If yes, explain. If no, write about why you think your friends have remained so faithful to you.

_____

_____

_____

_____

_____

_____

_____

_____

_____

_____

_____

Do you think having a "grief buddy"—someone else who is mourning a death that you can partner with in healing—would be helpful to you? If yes, write down a few people you could approach with this idea.

_____

_____

_____

_____

Nurturing Yourself: The Social Realm

Nurturing Yourself: The Spiritual Realm

How do you nurture your spirit?

_____

_____

_____

_____

_____

_____

_____

_____

_____

_____

_____

_____

Do you have a place where you can mourn and meditate in silence, all by yourself? Describe this place.

_____

_____

_____

_____

_____

_____

_____

_____

Do you pray? What do you pray for? Describe your prayer routine.

_____

_____

_____

_____

_____

_____

_____

_____

Would planting a special tree in honor of the person who died help you and others continue to heal? If yes, call someone today and discuss when and where to plant the tree and what kind of small ceremony you might have. If no, what other ritual might help you honor your grief and remember the person who died?

_____

_____

_____

_____

_____

_____

_____

_____

_____

Do you spend time in nature? If yes, how does it make you feel?

_____

_____

_____

_____

_____

_____

_____

Do you believe in heaven? If you do, close your eyes and imagine the person who died in heaven. What is it like? Write about this image here.

_____

_____

_____

_____

_____

_____

_____

_____

Free Write

Touchstone Eight
Reach Out for Help

In this chapter in the companion text…

We emphasized that healing in grief requires the support and understanding of those around you as you embrace the pain of your loss. You
cannot make this journey alone. We also discussed where you can turn
for help and how to tell if you need professional help. Finding and
working with a grief counselor was explored, as was finding and
working with a grief support group.

List three people you have reached out to for support thus far in your grief journey and describe the ways in which they have helped you:

1._____
This person has helped me by ...

_____

_____

_____

_____

_____

_____

_____

2._____
This person has helped me by ...

_____

_____

_____

_____

_____

_____

_____

3._____
This person has helped me by ...

_____

_____

_____

_____

_____

_____

_____

Do you have close friends and compassionate family members who will be your companions on your journey through grief? If yes, write about who these family members are and how they help you. If no, write about where else you might seek support.

_____

_____

_____

_____

_____

_____

_____

_____

_____

Is there a clergyperson or other spiritual leader you could turn to for help? If so, who?

_____

_____

_____

_____

_____

_____

_____

Have you located a professional counselor to see or a support group to attend? If so, you'll be asked to describe them later in this journal chapter. If no, explore why you haven't felt the need or desire to seek out a counselor or support group.

_____

_____

_____

Where to Turn for Help

The Rule of Thirds

The rule of thirds says that when you're in grief, you'll typically find that about one-third of the people in your life will be a help to you, one-third will neither help nor harm you, and one-third will be a hindrance to your healing. Below, identify the one-third you believe will be a help to you in your journey through grief.

_____

_____

_____

_____

_____

_____

_____

_____

_____

_____

_____

_____

_____

_____

_____

_____

_____

_____

How Others Can Help You

Who helps you feel hopeful?

_____

_____

Who listens to you "tell your story" and recount the pain of your loss?

_____

_____

Who helps you feel, in general, companioned on your grief journey?

_____

_____

As you read about the factors that could complicate your grief, did you find some of them that would apply to you and your situation? If so, which one(s)? Please explain.

_____

_____

_____

_____

_____

_____

_____

How to Know if You Need Professional Help

Have you noticed any of the behavior patterns in yourself that might indicate complicated grief? If so, which one(s)? Please explain.

_____

_____

_____

_____

_____

_____

_____

Signs of Complicated Grief

Note: if you are severely depressed, considering or planning suicide, or abusing drugs or alcohol, please talk to someone right now about your problems. You may write about them in this journal, as well, but to help yourself and protect those you love, you must also talk to someone you trust. It is also appropriate to call 911 if your life is in immediate danger. You are precious! Get the help you deserve!

How to Find A Good Counselor

If you have looked into seeing a grief counselor, write down the possible names and phone numbers here.

_____

_____

_____

_____

_____

If you are seeing a counselor, take the inventory of questions on pp. 134-137 of *Understanding Your Grief*. Add up your score and note it here: _____ total points

Deciding If a Counselor is Right for You

If you feel you might need to find a different counselor, create an action plan here for doing so.

_____

_____

_____

_____

_____

_____

_____

_____

_____

_____

_____

_____

_____

_____

_____

_____

_____

If you are in counseling, describe below what the counseling experience is or has been like for you. If not, go on to the next page.

_____

_____

_____

_____

_____

_____

_____

_____

_____

_____

_____

_____

_____

_____

_____

_____

_____

_____

_____

_____

_____

_____

_____

_____

_____

How to Find A Support Group

Have you looked into finding and joining a grief support group? Make note of where you are in this process and what additional steps you need to take to get involved in a support group.

_____

_____

_____

_____

_____

_____

_____

_____

_____

_____

_____

_____

_____

How To Know If You've Found A "Healthy" Support Group

If you are currently or have been a member of a support group, re-read the criteria for a "healthy" support group on pp. 142-143. Now, in the space below, write about your group experience specifically as it relates to these criteria.

_____

_____

_____

_____

_____

_____

_____

_____

_____

_____

Free Write

Touchstone Nine
Seek Reconciliation, Not Resolution

In this chapter in the companion text…

We defined what it means to reconcile your grief instead of recovering from it or resolving it. We explained that as the experience of reconciliation unfolds, you will recognize that life is and will continue to be different without the presence of the person who died. Yet you will move forward in life with a renewed sense of energy and confidence, an ability to fully acknowledge the reality of the death, and a capacity to become re-involved in the activities of living. We also listed a number of "signs" that reconciliation is taking place in your journey. Finally, we explored the role of continued hope, trust, and faith in the achievement of reconciliation.

In the space below, take the opportunity to write out where you see yourself in your own unique healing process. As you have learned about the concept of reconciliation, what thoughts and feelings come to mind? Be compassionate with yourself if you are not as far along in your healing as you (or others) would like. After all, through reading *Understanding Your Grief* and completing this journal, you have certainly created some divine momentum in your healing.

_____

_____

_____

_____

_____

_____

_____

_____

_____

_____

_____

_____

_____

_____

Signs of Reconciliation

Which, if any, of the listed signs of reconciliation are you seeing in yourself right now? Note them here.

_____

_____

_____

_____

_____

_____

_____

_____

_____

In the space below, write out what you are doing or have done to help yourself move toward reconciliation.

_____

_____

_____

_____

_____

_____

_____

_____

_____

_____

_____

_____

Signs of Reconciliation (cont.)

Do you have hope for your healing? Explain.

_____

_____

_____

_____

_____

_____

_____

_____

_____

_____

_____

_____

_____

Hope for Your Healing

Hope for Your Healing (cont.)

Does your faith sustain you in your journey to reconciliation in grief? Explain.

_____

_____

_____

_____

_____

_____

_____

_____

_____

_____

_____

_____

Do you believe that life continues after death? Explain how this affects your journey to reconciliation in grief.

_____

_____

_____

_____

_____

_____

_____

_____

_____

_____

_____

_____

_____

_____

_____

Free Write

Touchstone Ten

Appreciate Your Transformation

In this chapter in the companion text...

We affirmed that the journey through grief is life-changing and that when you leave the wilderness of your grief, you are simply not the same person as when you entered the wilderness. We also recognized that the transformation you see in yourself—and the personal growth you are experiencing as a result of the death—are not changes you would masochistically seek out. The fact that you are indeed trans- formed does not mean you are grateful the person died. Still, we explored the various ways in which people grow through grief. We suggested that you must live not only for yourself, but also for the precious person in your life who has died. We also asked you to consider how you can most authentically live your transformed life from here forward.

How are you discovering that you are being transformed by your grief?

_____
_____
_____
_____
_____
_____
_____
_____
_____
_____
_____
_____
_____

What changes have you seen in yourself (new attitudes, insights, skills) since the death?

_____
_____
_____
_____
_____
_____
_____

Have you found or are you in the process of finding a new inner balance or a "new normal?" Please explain.

_____
_____
_____
_____
_____

Growth Means Change/A New Inner Balance

Have your values changed since the death? If so, how?

_____

_____

_____

_____

_____

_____

_____

_____

How has your view of God and spirituality changed since the death?

_____

_____

_____

_____

_____

_____

_____

_____

Do you believe you have a purpose in life? If so, what is it? If not, why not?

_____

_____

_____

_____

_____

_____

_____

_____

Growth Means Exploring Your Assumptions/Utilizing Your Potential

How are you making use of your potential?

_____

_____

_____

_____

_____

_____

_____

_____

Your Responsibility To Live

Do you believe that you have a responsibility to live, in part, on behalf of the person who died? If yes, why? If no, why not?

_____

_____

_____

_____

_____

_____

_____

_____

What could you do in your present and future life to honor the life of the person who died?

_____

_____

_____

_____

_____

_____

_____

_____

Name one specific thing you could do today to honor the person's unfinished contributions to the world:

_____

_____

_____

How do you nourish your transformed soul? List the ways here.

_____

_____

_____

_____

_____

_____

_____

_____

Nourishing Your Transformed Soul

How will you most authentically live your transformed life?

_____

_____

_____

_____

_____

_____

_____

_____

_____

_____

_____

_____

_____

Free Write

Continuing Your Journey

In the months and years to come, I invite you to revisit this book and reflect on the ongoing and ever-changing nature of your journey through grief. How is your grief changing? How do you know you are achieving reconciliation in your grief? In what ways do you see yourself continuing to transform? Please take a moment now and then to jot down updates in the blank pages that follow. Shalom.